GOD BLESS THE CHILD

WORDS AND MUSIC BY **Billie Holiday** AND **Arthur Herzog Jr.**

ILLUSTRATED BY **Jerry Pinkney**

HARPERCOLLINSPUBLISHERS · Amistad

Amistad is an imprint of HarperCollins Publishers Inc.

God Bless the Child
Words and music copyright © 1941 by Edward B. Marks Music Company.
Copyright renewed. Used by permission. All rights reserved. Illustrations copyright © 2004 by Jerry Pinkney
Printed in the U.S.A.
All rights reserved. www.harperchildrens.com

Library of Congress Cataloging-in-Publication Data

Holiday, Billie, 1915–1959.
 God bless the child / words and music by Billie Holiday and Arthur Herzog Jr. ; illustrated by Jerry Pinkney.
  p.   cm.
 Summary: A swing spiritual based on the proverb "God blessed the child that's got his own."
 ISBN 0-06-028797-7—ISBN 0-06-029487-6 (lib. bdg.)
 1. Children's songs—United States—Texts. [1. Spirituals (Songs) 2. Songs.] I. Herzog, Arthur, Jr.
II. Pinkney, Jerry, ill. III. Title.
PZ8.3.H4377 Go 2004
782.42164'0268—dc21
[E]
                                                                                            00-063200

Typography by Matt Adamec   1 2 3 4 5 6 7 8 9 10   ❖   First Edition

In memory of Billie Holiday,
whose music gave voice to our deepest emotions,
and of Jacob Lawrence and his Great Migration series,
which inspired my vision for this book

I would like to thank Gloria Jean Pinkney for all her help, especially in locating the models to portray the characters in this book. She found the perfect subjects for my rural family. I would like to thank Rosemary Wells as well for bringing me to this project, and I would also like to express my appreciation to Oyekunie Oyegbemi of the Mississippi Project and to the staff members at the Du Sable Museum of African American History, the Chicago Historical Society, Alcorn State University, and the Croton Free Library, who were so helpful with my research into the Great Migration.

Them that's got shall get,
Them that's not shall lose,
So the Bible said,
And it still is news;

Mama may have,
Papa may have,
But God bless the child
That's got his own!
That's got his own.

Yes, the strong gets more,
While the weak ones fade,
Empty pockets don't ever make the grade;

Mama may have,
Papa may have,
But God bless the child
That's got his own!
That's got his own.

Money, you got lots o' friends,
Crowdin' round the door,
When you're gone and spendin' ends,
They don't come no more.

Rich relations give,
Crust of bread, and such,
You can help yourself,
But don't take too much!

Mama may have,
Papa may have,
But God bless the child
That's got his own!
That's got his own.

ARTIST'S NOTE

For some time now, I have been collecting books of vintage photographs of people of African descent, which has resulted in an extensive visual reference library documenting the African American experience over the past one hundred fifty years. As I searched for a vision to illustrate Billie Holiday and Arthur Herzog Jr.'s "God Bless the Child," it was these arresting images that came to mind, particularly the many photographs that reveal a proud and industrious people. It was these that started me down a path of inquiry that led to images of the African American sharecroppers of the Deep South, and to their Great Migration.

The Great Migration began around 1900 and continued well into the 1950s. It was the largest peacetime movement of people in the United States, reaching its peak during the 1930s. Spurred by tales of higher-paying jobs, free schooling, and good living conditions, thousands of folks moved from fading rural plantations to Chicago and other promising cities in the industrialized North. Whole families picked up and moved, taking only what they could carry on the train, bundle into their wagons, or tie onto their automobiles. They fled failing crops, exploitation, and unrealized dreams with unwavering hope for a better life.

But starting fresh in a strange city was not easy. The new arrivals had to find housing, employment, and acceptance by city-dwellers, both white and black, and the migrants soon realized that the long shadow of segregation had followed them up north.

Music followed them, too. People packed up spirituals and folksongs like valued possessions and carried them along as nourishment for their souls. This down-home music mingled with urban jazz in the northern cities, and gave rise to great blues singers such as Billie Holiday and songs such as "God Bless the Child."

No book gets made without research, and for this story I spent hours with library and museum staff members looking into photographic records of the 1930s. I was also fortunate to be able to discuss the Great Migration with people who had experienced it firsthand. Their personal perspectives were an invaluable inspiration.

This story ends in a classroom. At the time "God Bless the Child" was written, education was largely a privilege of the wealthy. Children of the poor were expected to work alongside their parents to put food on the table, and for a child of the Great Migration, going to school would have seemed like a dream come true. Free public education was prized as the great equalizer—the stairway out of poverty for those with the courage and the opportunity to climb it.

On the blackboard we see the name Jean Baptiste Point Du Sable, a person of color. This eighteenth-century merchant, fur trader, and farmer loomed large in the formative history of Chicago, the city that was the goal of so many Great Migration pilgrims.

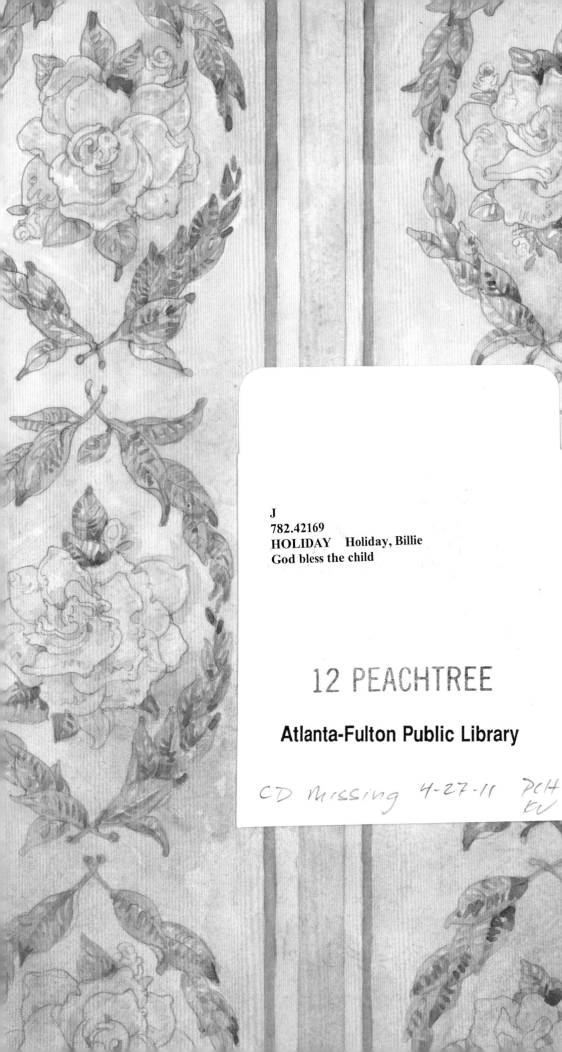